HEAD

LAND

Foreword

Limerick City Gallery of Art (LCGA) is delighted to be the originator of this wonderful exhibition, Headland, of new and recent work by Elizabeth Magill. Many years have passed since Elizabeth has had an exhibition in a public institution in Ireland and I am really proud that LCGA has corrected this oversight. This exhibition provides a wonderful opportunity for us to work with one of Ireland's foremost painters.

The apparent lightness of touch in Magill's paintings belies the depth of the images and its need to seek out, probe, examine and constantly look with a steady and fearless gaze. The elision of past and present of public history and private memories, of shared experiences and unique responses is typical of Magill's work. First encounters with Elizabeth Magill's work can seem apparently easy to read but a closer reading reveals much of her own history and sensitivity, her connection to the landscape of her native County Antrim, to other artists and their influences on her work both directly and indirectly and to constantly seeking bold ways to express her painting.

The exhibition received an Arts Council *Touring and Dissemination of Work Scheme* award which has enabled us to tour the show to the RHA, Dublin. It will also tour to the Ulster Museum, Belfast and The New Art Gallery, Walsall, UK in 2018.

Anthony Wilkinson of Anthony Wilkinson Gallery, London has been an inestimable support in the preparation of this exhibition and the co-ordination of the catalogue. Enormous thanks to Isobel Harbison and Tom Nys who have written so eloquently and perceptively on Magill's work. Deserving of my sincere gratitude are the patience and interest of the amazing team at LCGA most especially Siobhan O'Reilly and Ger Moloney. I also want to acknowledge the wider public whose support of LCGA allows us to push the artistic boundaries. I wish to thank Kerlin Gallery, Dublin for their input into the realisation of this exhibition. Finally I wish to acknowledge the continued support of Limerick City and County Council.

Headland is an exquisite exhibition, with compelling new work. My sincere thanks to Patrick Murphy, Director of the RHA, Anne Stewart, Curator of Fine Art, Ulster Museum and Stephen Snoddy, Director of The New Art Gallery, Walsall. Finally thank you to the private collectors and institutions who have made work available for inclusion in this exhibition.

Above all my sincere thanks to Elizabeth Magill for her belief in us and for working so patiently and generously to ensure that we could reacquaint people with her work and introduce a new generation to the "hours and miles and joys" of Headland.

Úna McCarthy
Director/Curator
LCGA
December 2017

Goat Song, 2010-2017
Oil on canvas, 26 x 30 cm

A bluff, a rock, a hole in the ground

'The center of the world is a bluff on the Klamath River, a rock in Mecca, a hole in the ground in Greece, nowhere, its circumference everywhere. Perhaps the utopist should heed this unsettling news at last', Ursula K. Le Guin wrote in 1982, about post-colonial theory's dismantling of the 'White West'. Around that time Elizabeth Magill moved from rural County Antrim to London, a city of bricks and slabs and debris where she began painting bluffs and rocks and holes, but the landscapes she presents are neither romantic nor utopian. John Berger writes 'to emigrate is always to dismantle the centre of the world, and so to move into a lost, disorientated one of fragments', and her works might be considered a perpetual, partial return to a homeland as a way of reflecting upon a world that is fragmented, fractured and parched and, ultimately, the artist's role in traversing it.

Magill's work brings together photography and painting, media that have historically produced new ways of imagining as they have changed our means of seeing – of connecting with – one another and the ground beneath us. In many of her works painting and photography converge to render the limits of one another, and to test the boundary between the world and the images that bring it to us. *Divide* (2017) is a small oil and film on canvas that does this most explicitly, where thick strokes of pink impasto in the centre of the composition push against the lips of prints of tall ferns pasted to both sides of the painting's vertical margins. Paint pushes back from the precipice to fight its place as a central mode of reproduction among mechanical alternatives, emphasizing its capacity to render human touch, or rather the concerted and considerable impact on that which we touch.

The tree is a dendriform structure that repeats throughout her *oeuvre,* often planted between central middle-ground and the ground of the spectator like a forth wall. The dendriform is also emblematic of branches of thought, cerebral passageways, through ways and byways, memories undergoing constant mutation and change. *Headland* (2017) depicts a landmass projecting from the coastline in the middle distance surrounded by a lake in wash of shades of pink and blue and yellow. Dark trees stand in the painting's foreground. These foreground figures are printed with screenprint on canvas, first yellow then overlaid with black so what appears is a sliver of light to the right of the bark. We're locked out of the centre of this composition, excluded from the light, on the tree's dark side. This is not a Romantic landscape where natural elements guide the eye towards a central point but rather flatten and fortify the foreground to shut the viewer out. It's a partial view of a space that is not entirely ours to visit.

Magill's colour palette and light effects are very specific: dark, enigmatic landscapes with shivers of pinks, yellows and blue. There is a chemical toxicity to these shades that inflect landscapes so that they are suggestive and recognizable but non-naturalistic, or perhaps, post-natural. Which is not to say she paints a world that has transcended or gone beyond nature, but rather one that's undergoing a transition, the outcome of which is still uncertain. Magill's pink headland juts out in a landscape erased of life, leaving an image of what poet Frances Ferguson coined as the 'nuclear sublime'. Transcriptions by General Thomas Farrell of the first US atomic bombs in 1945 attempt to find language for a situation where 'the whole country was lighted by a searing light with the intensity many times of the midday sun... golden, purple, violet, gray and blue. It lighted every peak, crevasse, and mountain range with a clarity and beauty that cannot be described but must be seen to be imagined'. Reading Farrell's stunned account, Rob Wilson registered 'a terrifying abyss', between cognition (the language of the self) and its corresponding object (nature sublimated into atomic energy).

Formally and tonally, Magill's paintings connect canals of thought with the physical surrounds on which such thought has consequence. In *Red Bay* (2016-17), Magill adopts a similar format to *Headland*. It is a coastal scene, looking out to sea from a bay with a sky of grey and blue breaking out with silvery light. A rain shower seems to have just passed. In the background to the right, a dark headland sits up from the coast. But between the foreground and the wet beach hang the branches of a tree, this time a deep red and reaching down from the top margin, rather than sprouting from the canvas base. We're held here again with restricted access to the partial view. This is the picture of a bay in County Antrim, Northern Ireland. It is an image without violence from a region long familiar with trauma and the shade of the branches appear like a ghostly imprint, streaming down like rivulets of blood. Behind the branch a walker strides along the beach, head tilted against the wind. Magill rarely introduces figures and when she does they seem part of the atmosphere rather than a focal point. She aims for her figures to "have the same weight as a cloud, or a tree, or a bird, the same compositional value." Here, that presence is evoked through small scale and tone, printed in feint gray, distant and more translucent than the bold headland or red branches. He or she might be the specter of the artist on an imagined return.

Magill's paintings are epic, enigmatic and evocative and might be interestingly associated with many genres of painterly film, from the 'photogenié' of French

Impressionism, to the foreboding monochromes of Hollywood Noire, to the surface crackle and flicker of experimental film, but something of her predisposition towards celestial journeymen, dark ambiance and sinister spaces resonate with Soviet Science Fiction. Tarkovsky's 'Stalker' (1979) is a science fiction thriller set in an undisclosed year and city, following a troubled writer and determined science professor as they make their way to an infamous 'Zone' on the city's periphery. In the Zone there's a room where any desires of those who enter will be fulfilled, but the journey to it is so full of invisible threats only perceptible through the senses, they employ a guide or 'stalker'. Many of its central scenes were shot in deserted power plants and chemical factories around Tallinn, a toxicity that ultimately, allegedly, killed many of the film crew. When, several years later, the Chernobyl disaster hit, it was called the 'Zone of Alienation' and those who entered illegally to clear or see the debris identified as 'stalkers'. The Zone is a potentially poisonous post-nuclear area, but people risk contamination to get to its room. Tarkovsky's room is an imaginary space, and a space for the imaginary, that might be interpreted as a metonym for avant-garde film and its place against Cold War paranoia and a crumbling Soviet regime.

Explorers appear throughout Magill's work, in *Trio Edge* (2016), three dark figures creep across the land, silhouetted beneath a shady galaxy. They could be anyone from anywhere, so shrouded they are in darkness, but they lean forward, battling against the elements or the undergrowth or other unseen forces. They are on a mission. They might be Tarkovsky's trio in search of his imaginary room. In *Gazers* (2016), two savants cross the canvas in the other direction, walking towards the right background. The figures have been collaged on from a painting of Greek Orthodox monks retreating into cenobitic life in a lavra. In her canvas, there is no architectural ground. Instead the pale figures are suspended in the dark, surrounded by vertical paint strokes in mossy shades with highlights of bright blue and yellow, lines that surge or spout around these figures like strange cosmic beams. In one figure's hand sits an orb, echoed by smaller white orbs painted floating around them. And this figure is echoed too by a duplicate cutout silhouette beside it, but this one subdued in colour beneath more mossy shades. This is a picture of enigmatic nomads, of timeless, genderless savants forging onwards, and of the process, endeavor and sanctum of continued reflection. Despite obscene human violence, on the brink of nuclear warfare, when we know our ecologies are damaged but unsure whether they're beyond repair, when the world is dirty and Western epistemology de-centred, Magill's explorers symbolize the human instinct of continual exploration however fractured the ground beneath.

Magill's works offer ruminations on painting – on *art* – and its place and role in a catastrophe-laden, post-natural world. *Hogsland* (2015-16) is a painting of Henry Moore's studio in Herefordshire seen through several crops of trees. The studio building looks like a shelter or hut where panels replace windows or doors, leaning together. It appears neither fragile nor robust, but rather modifiable: the ad hoc infrastructures that sustained practice and applied thinking builds. The studio is partially concealed by clusters of trees, tall grand firs to the right foreground, to the left some birch, scorched or spared their leaves, and all of which grow from a dark green mossy bed. These trees are again painted over time, their styles and paint handling quite different, the firs rich and green and delicately figured, the birch are leafless, more angular and abstract. From the paint surface, it's clear they've come in to being gradually, and stand between the artist's retreat and the viewer before it. They accent the artist's process, her commitment to formal experimentation, to trial and trial, to thought and rethinking, articulated over time. The piece is influenced by Henry David Thoreau's novel, 'Walden; or, Life in the Woods' (1854), and his transcendental reflection on a solitary, 'Spartan-like' survival in rural isolation written over a two-year retreat to a cottage beside Walden Pond in Massachusetts in 1854. There's a reflection on making art within *Hogsland*, of isolating and extracting oneself from the familiar, of enduring and surviving the zone in order to reach the room, a space for the imaginary, a headland, and of remaining there over long periods in processes of looking and learning, despite all odds.

Isobel Harbison

Sea Green 2016
Oil on canvas, 20.5 x 25.5 cm

Trio Edge 2016
Oil on canvas and glitter, 20.5 x 25.5 cm

Plot 2017
Oil on canvas, 20.5 x 25.5 cm

Of (2), 2017
Oil and screenprint on paper
145 x 185 cm

Sulphur, 2017
Oil and screenprint on paper
139.5 x 173 cm

Unstill, 2017
Oil and screenprint on aluminium mounted paper
145 x 185 cm

Neck, 2017
Oil and screenprint on aluminium mounted paper
185 x 145 cm

Descend, 2017
Oil and screenprint on paper
145 x 185 cm

Along, 2017
Oil and screenprint on paper
145 x 185 cm

Red Bay, 2016-2017
Oil and screenprint on canvas
153 x 183.5 cm

Anterior (1), 2017
Oil and screenprint on canvas
153 x 183 cm

Headland (1), 2017
Oil and screenprint on canvas
153 x 183.5 cm

Wildlife, 2017
Oil and screenprint on canvas
153 x 183.5 cm

Multi-Storey, 2017
Oil and screenprint on canvas
153 x 183 cm

Still (2), 2017
Oil and screenprint on canvas
183 x 153 cm

Still (1), 2017
Oil and screenprint on canvas
183 x 153

Irrawaddy, 2017
Oil and screenprint on canvas
153 x 183 cm

After Earth, 2016
Oil on canvas
153 x 183 cm

Only Tune, 2016
Oil and charcoal on canvas
153 x 183 cm

Return, 2016
Oil and collage on canvas
153 x 183 cm

Gazers, 2016
Oil and collage on canvas
26 x 26.5 cm

Hogsland, 2015-2016
Oil on canvas
153 x 183 cm

Blue Rise and Then 2016
Oil & film on canvas
22.5 x 31.5 cm

Berlin 2016
Oil & film on canvas
22.5 x 31.5 cm

View Point (2) 2017
Oil & film on canvas
22.5 x 31.5 cm

Stalker Moon 2016
Oil & film on canvas
22.5 x 31.5 cm

Divide 2017
Oil & film on canvas
22.5 x 31.5 cm

Roches & Richter 2017
Oil & film on canvas
22.5 x 31.5 cm

History Boat 2016
Oil & film on canvas
22.5 x 31.5 cm

Cezanne's House (2) 2016
Oil & film on canvas
22.5 x 31.5 cm

Demoiselles 2015-17
Oil & film on canvas
22.5 x 31.5 cm

Cezannes' House (1) 2016
Oil & film on canvas
22.5 x 31.5 cm

Walden 2016
Oil & film on canvas
22.5 x 31.5 cm

Mid Way 2016
Oil & film on canvas
22.5 x 31.5 cm

Painting is, in essence, an act of accumulating beds of paint or a pigmented substance onto a carrier surface. Despite modernism's preoccupation with the two-dimensionality of paintings, the moment a line, dot, patch or brushstroke touches the chosen ground and finally solidifies, the notion of flatness has been impaired. As the layers of paint amass, the painting as object protrudes further into space, an idea that at a certain point in art history was pushed to its limits, for instance by introducing real objects onto the surface.

Paradoxically, this superposition of paint very often (co)produces a sensation of depth, and in the case of figurative art, this impression will be enhanced by the use of perspective. The painting establishes interplay between the space it contains and the space it is surrounded by, which is ultimately the interactive space of the viewer. Moreover, there are ample of examples of traditions in art history that specifically exploit this trait, such as the use of *repoussoir* figures or *tromp-l'oeil* images. Notice also, how people talk about what is *in* a painting, rather than *on* it, the latter preposition being more generally used when describing abstract works.

Elizabeth Magill explicitly engages in accruing and juxtaposing layers in diverse techniques, materials, textures and degrees of abstraction, until a coherent representation, often populated by figures and symbols, materialises. Indeed, in her work, accumulation takes place on three levels: that of the factual, pictorial spatiality, that of techniques and that of symbols. This rigorous layering is worth analysing more closely.

Thus, it will become evident that in each one of Magill's paintings, the bottom layer, which rests directly upon the undercoat, is a kaleidoscopic plane, invariably fluid or ethereal in appearance and seemingly expanding outside the limits of the canvas. It may comprise several areas that are different in colour or in tactility, sometimes colliding, in other instances gradual. This all-over quality is the result of a laborious, gestural process that involves the pouring, blending, dripping and splashing of paint on a canvas that has been laid out on the studio floor. While this indisputably invites a chance effect, the artist, who has perfected this modus operandi over the years, has always proven herself to be in control during the process.

Significantly, the applied hues are frequently soft and subdued, even the darker tones, and they are able to emanate a time in-between day and night. It might be a sultry dusk or a chilling dawn, one is never quite sure. This timely in-betweenness is crucial, as it reinforces the dreamlike nature of the depicted. It is on top of this stratum, when it has finally sedimented and

established itself to the liking of the artist, that several layers embedded with meaning will be compiled.

The setting of Magill's preference is, as we know, the landscape, which she treats in a great variety of ways. Of course, a landscape as a representation is already a composition in every sense of the word, particularly in a painted form. While the word landscape signifies both the referent as its representation, landscape painters, with the exception of naturalists, pleinairists or photorealists, generally compromise the relationship between the two, altering and expanding on the canvas what is observed or imagined.

This is done to some extent to meet stylistic conventions and a standard set of laws, a canon that photography and cinema at first followed rigidly too. Gradually, the latter media generated many revolutions within the genre definitions of western landscape painting, introducing new perspectives, viewpoints, framing methods and so forth. Magill's landscapes bare witness of these paradigm shifts, as they confront the viewer with typically photographic or cinematic takes on the genre. What is more, the incorporation of the screenprint technique or the plastic film medium in several works gives away the artist's fascination for photos and film. In addition, it enhances the hybrid character of those paintings, in terms of their style as well as their phenomenology.

Subsequently, Magill directs the viewer with a wide array of pictorial means through a forest of symbols, to paraphrase Charles Baudelaire, that watch him/her with familiar glances. Her imagery originates from sundry sources: an exhaustive personal collection of photographs, imagery taken from books and magazines, reproductions and most important of all her own memory. In any case, we do not wander through these symbolic forests alone, while the human as well as the animal form are commonly present, or implied. These figures emerge distantly or ghostly, like the running girl, the two women with the long dresses, the couple walking hand in hand or the mountain hikers from another time. Evidence of human presence or cultural artefacts can be recurrently perceived, such as boats, roads and buildings. In fact, the architecture is rarely urban or metropolitan, rather rural and solitary.

Fishman, 2014-2015
Oil and screenprint on canvas
198 x 167.5 cm

Les Demoiselles, 2014-2015
Oil on canvas
183 x 153 cm

And typically, like the paintings' personages, these man-made artefacts and structures do not dominate the scene visually, they have an air of being phantasmal or adrift, referencing their status as floating signifiers.

On several works produced in the last few years, fragments that reference a few illustrious paintings from western art history are recognisable. They particularly look as if they were collaged into Magill's own universe, and are trying to integrate themselves into it. This type of allusion is indeed relatively new to Magill. Displaced from their original context, their symbolic load is transformed and assimilated into a scene imagined by the artist. For instance, Picasso's seminal *bordel*, now known as 'Les Demoiselles d'Avignon' (1907), a gathering of *belles-de-nuit* who he represented in a very sculptural manner, figures in a few of Magill's artworks. It may act as homage, as a mere motif or as a vehicle for addressing particular ideas. What is obvious, though, is that in Magill's version (2015-7), the women, who are now placed in-between numerous trees that intersect the small painting's plane, seem even more objectified and statuesque. In another rendering from 2014-15, they are deconstructed even further and become part of a scrambled image in various blues, resembling a cameo-effect and coming close to the abstract.

Another example is *Fishman* (2014-15), which puts central a figure that might be lesser known: it is derived from a 1969 sculpture by American artist Paul Thek, with the same title. Magill has put the anthropomorphic shape in similar dimensions as the trees she painted around it, offering a plethora of understandings. Yet in the case of *Cezanne's House* (2016), of which Magill made two different versions, an unmistakable clue is incorporated. Based on a depiction of a house in the province that the French artist painted when he, in later life, returned to the region where he spent most of his childhood, one can easily discern the significance in relation to Magill's own personal trajectory, being more and more susceptible to the call of the Irish land.

Unsurprisingly, picturesque parts of Northern Ireland constitute an imperative constituent of Magill's landscapes, like for instance Garron Point, which features on *Red Bay* (2015-17), *Sulphur* (2017) as well as on *Headland (1)* (2017). Although the artist spent some of her early childhood in Canada, where she was born, and has resided in London for many years, Ireland, homeland of her parents, is still in her blood. Nowadays, she regularly stays for longer periods in a cottage near the coastline, a setting familiar to those who have seen enough of her work. Moreover, other motifs employed by Magill have a background in Irish history, architecture, and folk tales.

Corot London, 2015-2017
Oil on canvas
31 x 31 cm

Head, 2004-2017
Oil on canvas
31 x 31 cm

Oberland 2017
Oil and screenprint on canvas
183.5 x 153 cm / 153 x 183.5 cm

The accumulation of layers does not stop here, though, as Magill is keen on bestowing large, painted parts of trees, trunks and brushwood in front of the centre of a piece, making the work more akin to a film still or photograph than to a traditional landscape painting. By obstructing and even concealing the central view in this way, one has to draw closer to read the whole image properly; it even generates a scopophilic or voyeuristic stance. Thus, this superimposed layer establishes a different kind of relationship with the corporeality of the viewer. It engages a person standing in front of the painting in his or her interactional territory and draws them into the depiction. In several works, the artist even adds yet another stratum, a film that seems to have been laid over the entire image. It may contain faint brushstrokes, dots of paint or symbols such as numbers. Again, Magill uses another approach to complicate a direct interpretation of the whole work.

By now, it has become clear how the artist brings into play the idea of accumulation on different levels and in various layers. Her works are compilations, constructions and, quite literally, compositions. Composed of elements born out of her imagination, we might conclude that Magill's landscapes are in fact *inscapes*. Accordingly, the title "Headland" can be read in such a way too. Even here, the obfuscation cleverly continues.

Tom Nys, 2017.

Elizabeth Magill

Born in Canada. Lives and works in London and N. Ireland.

1979-82 Belfast College of Art, Fine Art Degree, Painting

1982-84 Slade School of Art, University College London;
MA Painting

Selected Solo Exhibitions

2018   Matts Gallery, London

2017-18 *Headland*, Limerick City Gallery of Art, Limerick;
Royal Hibernian Academy, Dublin;
Ulster Museum, Belfast;
The New Art Gallery Walsall (cat.)

2017   *Headland*, Wilkinson Gallery, London

2013   *Quasi-Real & Branch-Like*,
Wilkinson Gallery, London

2010-11 *Green Light Wanes*, Towner Art Gallery,
Eastbourne & Kerlin Gallery, Dublin (cat.)

2009   *Elizabeth Magill & John Frankland*,
The Russian Club Studios, London

2008   *Chronicle of Orange*, Wilkinson Gallery, London (cat.)

2006   *Arborescence*, Kerlin Gallery, Dublin

2004/5 *Elizabeth Magill* (touring exhibition), Ikon Gallery,
Birmingham; Milton Keynes Gallery,
Milton Keynes; BALTIC, Gateshead;
Glynn Vivian Gallery, Swansea (cat.)

2003   *New Works*, Artemis Greenberg Van Doren,
New York NY (cat.)

Elizabeth Magill, Hugh Lane Municipal Gallery,
Dublin

Galerie Ghislaine Hussenot, Paris

2002   Anthony Wilkinson Gallery, London

2001   Gallery Deux, Tokyo, Japan

Peer Gallery, Peer Trust, London

1999   Kerlin Gallery, Dublin

Elizabeth Magill, Painting, Southampton City Art
Gallery, Southampton (cat.)

1997   Galerie 102, Dusselsorf, Germany

1995   Saarlandisches Kuenstlerhaus, Saarbrucken,
Germany (cat.)

1994   *Freds Leap*, Bluecoat Gallery, Liverpool

1992   *Belongings*, Kerlin Gallery, Dublin

1991   Emilio Navarro Gallery, Madrid (cat.)

1990   *Elizabeth Magill*, Arnolfini Gallery, Bristol (cat.)

Selected Group Exhibitions

2017   *Legacies JMW Turner and contemporary art practice*, The New Art Gallery Walsall

2016   *A Certain Kind of Light*, Towner Art Gallery, Eastbourne.

2015   *Artists for Ikon*, Ikon Gallery, Birmingham, UK

2014-13   *Under the Green Wood*, Gerald Moore Gallery, London & St Barbe Museum, Lymington

2012   *John Moores Painting Prize Exhibition*, Walker Art Gallery, Liverpool

       Landscape, Hite Collection, Artsonje Centre, Seoul, Korea

       Time out of Mind, Irish Museum of Art, Dublin

2011   *Interlude*, Douglas Hyde Gallery, Dublin

2009   *Known Unknown*, Gallery Loop, Seoul, Korea

       Skies, Nottingham Museum & Art Gallery, Nottingham

2008   *There not There*, Crawford Museum, Cork

       10,000 to 50, Contemporary Art, IMMA, Dublin

2006   *No Answer is Also an Answer*, Dublin City Gallery, The Hugh Lane, (cat.)

2006   *Out of Place*, The New Art Gallery, Walsall

2005   *Siar*, IMMA, Dublin

2004   *Landscape 2*, Towner Art Gallery & Museum, Eastbourne

2002   *Something Else* (touring exhibition), Turku Art Museum, Turku, Finland (cat.)

2001   *I Love Melancholy*, Northern Gallery of Contemporary Art, Sunderland & Southampton City Art Gallery

       IMMA/Glen Dimplex Exhibition, Irish Museum of Modern Art, Dublin (cat.)

       Shifting Ground: Fifty Years of Irish Art, Irish Museum of Modern Art, Dublin (cat.)

2000   *Places in Mind*, Elizabeth Magill/Adam Chodzko/ Stan Douglas, Ormeau Baths Gallery, Belfast (cat.)

       Primio Michetti 2000, Fondazione Michetti, Italy (cat.)

1999   *0044*, PS1, New York and Albright-Knox Art Gallery, Buffalo

       Ormeau Baths Gallery, Belfast; Crawford Municipal Art Gallery, Cork (cat.)

1996   *Irsk 96*, *Kulturfest*, Arhus Kunstbyoning, Arhus, Denmark (cat.)

1995   *IMMA/Glen Dimplex* Artists Award, Irish Museum of Modern (cat.)

1992   *New Voices*, British Council Touring Exhibition 1992 -1997 (cat.)

       Whitechapel Open, Whitechapel Art Gallery, London

       Welcome Europe, Holsoboro Kunstmuseum, Denmark (cat.)

1991   *A View of London*, Salzburg Kunstverein, Austria (cat.)

1990   *The British Art Show*, McLennan Galleries, Glasgow, Leeds City Art Gallery, Hayward Gallery, London (cat.)

       Decoy, Serpentine Gallery, London (cat.)

Collections

Allied Irish Bank

Arts Council England

Arts Council of Northern Ireland

Arts Council of Ireland

Bank of Ireland

British Council

British Museum

Contemporary Art Society, Winter Garden Museum, Hull

Crawford Museum, Cork

Deutsche Bank

Dublin City Gallery, The Hugh Lane

Government Art Collection London

Guinness Peat Aviation

HSBC, UK

Irish Museum of Modern Art

Limerick City Gallery of Art

National Gallery of Australia

Neuberger Berman Collection, USA

The New Art Gallery, Walsall

Southampton City Art Gallery

Towner Art Gallery, Eastbourne

Ulster Museum, Belfast

University of Ulster, Belfast

Worcester Museum and Art Gallery

Installation view, Limerick City Gallery of Art, 2017

Elizabeth Magill would like to thank
the following especially Úna McCarthy, Siobhan O'Reilly
and staff at Limerick City Gallery of Art for their support
with hosting this exhibition and Anthony Wilkinson
for project managing this pubication

Also the following:

David Caines

Coriander Studios, Worton Hall, London

Dr Barbara Dawson

Hugo Glendinning

Isobel Harbison

Gill Hedley

Jeremy Hughes

Kerlin Gallery, Dublin

Patrick Murphy RHA

Tom Nys

Eamonn O'Mahoney, Studioworks

Dairne O'Sullivan, Public Relations

Stephen Snoddy, The New Art Gallery, Walsall

Anne Steward, Ulster Museum, Belfast

Richard and Debbi Burston, Tom Hall,
Stuart and Bianca Roden, and other private collectors
who have kindly lent to the exhibitions.

Elizabeth Magill *Headland*

Photography by Hugo Glendinning and Peter White
Designed by David Caines Unlimited

ISBN 978-0-9927969-1-4